BOOK WORMS

Community Workers

A Plumber's Job

Niles Worthington

Cavendish
Square

New York

Published in 2016 by Cavendish Square Publishing, LLC
243 5th Avenue, Suite 136, New York, NY 10016

First Edition

Website: cavendishsq.com

This publication represents the opinions and views of the author based on his or her personal experience, knowledge, and research. The information in this book serves as a general guide only. The author and publisher have used their best efforts in preparing this book and disclaim liability rising directly or indirectly from the use and application of this book.

CPSIA Compliance Information: Batch #WS15CSQ

All websites were available and accurate when this book was sent to press.

Library of Congress Cataloging-in-Publication Data

Worthington, Niles.
A plumber's job / Niles Worthington.
pages cm. — (Community workers)
Includes bibliographical references and index.
ISBN 978-1-50260-434-7 (hardcover)
ISBN 978-1-50260-433-0 (paperback)
ISBN 978-1-50260-435-4 (ebook)
1. Plumbers—Juvenile literature. 2. Plumbing—Vocational guidance—Juvenile literature. I. Title.

TH6124.W676 2016
696'.1023—dc23

2014050272

Editorial Director: David McNamara
Editor: Fletcher Doyle
Copy Editor: Cynthia Roby
Art Director: Jeffrey Talbot
Designer: Alan Sliwinski
Senior Production Manager: Jennifer Ryder-Talbot
Production Editor: Renni Johnson

The photographs in this book are used by permission and through the courtesy of: JCI/Tom Gill, Getty Images, cover; fstop123/E+/Getty Images, 5; iStockphoto.com/RuslanDashinsky, 7; auremar/shutterstock.com, 9; Jason Dolly/E+/Getty Images, 11; Minerva Studio/shutterstock.com, 13; VGstockstudio/shutterstock.com, 15; Lisa F. Young/shutterstock.com, 17; Cornstock/Getty Images, 19; fstop13/E+/Getty Images, 21.

Printed in the United States of America

Contents

I am a plumber.

A plumber fixes water problems.

5

People call a plumber when there is a **leak**.

They need the plumber to come quickly.

6

7

Stopping a leak can be hard.

There may not be much room to work.

9

I clear **drainpipes**.

I use special tools to do this.

11

I hook up water heaters.

Now you can take a hot bath!

13

My **plunger** opens **clogged** toilets.

This is not always fun.

14

15

I **install** plumbing in new homes.

The pipes go in before the walls.

17

New pipes are made of plastic.

They are made to fit together.

18

19

It is fun to help people.

I like being a plumber!

21

New Words

clogged (KLOGGED) Filled or blocked so nothing can go through.

drainpipes (DRANE pipes) Pipes that carry water from your house to the sewer.

install (in-STAHL) To put something in so it works.

leak (LEEK) Water or gas escaping through a hole.

plunger (PLUN-jer) A rubber cup on a handle that clears toilets and drains.

22

Index

About the Author

Niles Worthington plays soccer and tennis, and enjoys writing children's books. He also works in his family's pharmacy, located outside of Chicago, Illinois.

About BOOKWORMS

Bookworms help independent readers gain reading confidence through high-frequency words, simple sentences, and strong picture/text support. Each book explores a concept that helps children relate what they read to the world in which they live.